Reflecting God

SPIRITUAL KEYS TO UNLOCK THE SUPERNATURAL YOU

Liz Wright

ISBN-13: 978-1-8381648-0-5

Cover design: Iain Gutteridge
Publisher: Liz Wright Ministries Ltd.

CONTENTS

DEDICATION

To Jesus,

My Lord and my song, my everything.

ACKNOWLEDGEMENTS

'Reflecting God' is the collective effort of an amazing group of people I am privileged to call my family and friends. Every person touched and transformed by the truths contained within this book are a part of your legacy too. I am so thankful for each one of you!

There are a few of you I want to give particular honour to:

My husband Wesley and daughter Faith. You are the treasure of my life! Thank you for all of your love and support. My life is rich because I have you.

Susan Wright my incredible friend, COO and the woman without whom this ministry would not be where it is today. Your love and unwavering belief in people changes lives. You are a gift to all who are privileged to call you a dear friend.

Mary King & Charles Kown. Your wisdom, brilliant creativity and experience have made 'Reflecting God' possible. Thank you for believing in this message as much as I do.

Our intercessors. Your deep love for Jesus coupled with many years of experience in prayer have made the way for this message to be released to the world. I honour and love each of you.

ENDORSEMENTS

Liz Wright is one of the most profound lovers of Jesus that God has raised up, not only as a cutting-edge mouthpiece for such a time as this, but a carrier of His manifest Glory. I believe this book 'Reflecting God' will take you on a journey of a lifetime toward and into the Highest Prize of life... Him!

Brian Guerin
Founding President, Bridal Glory International

Liz Wright is one of the most captivating and clear prophetic voices of our generation. Her words flow with poetic purity and eloquence, inviting the reader into a reality of sweetness and oneness with the Divine. Every sentence carries weight and depth, breaking open the heart to experience torrents of unconditional Love.

Several times contemplating the words of this book, I was absorbed into the Presence of God and had to stop reading. These words are alive and if you engage them, they will open your heart to new dimensions of the limitless life in Christ. Enjoy this priceless book!

Justin Abraham
Founder, Company of Burning Hearts

'Reflecting God' is such an important book. As Liz writes, the Spirit's ministry to glorify and reveal Jesus flows powerfully through every word. You will experience the impact of an immoveable plumb line of truth, set before us in each life-changing key. No matter what your life's journey may be, your beliefs or past difficulties in knowing Him more deeply, this book brings the glorious Person of Jesus Christ right before us.

Page after page, the plumb line of His relentless love for us is firmly established and becomes impossible to forget. Many books change lives, but Jesus, through the pages of this book, is fulfilling His ministry to utterly transform you in the power and security of His Love. Liz, it's a masterpiece. Well done my friend...

Julie Brown

Author, The Mantle of Purity

It's time to be awakened to who you REALLY are! Liz Wright has written a beautiful, identity-activation devotional for anyone who is ready for a revelatory recalibration. Read this book and expect an encounter with the love of God that ignites a fresh passion to engage Heaven and transform Earth.

Darren Stott

Lead Pastor, Seattle Revival Center

May this book be the doorway for you to experience, encounter and irrefutably know you have come into life-union with Jesus by witnessing the transfiguration of yourself into His perfect likeness. As the Spirit did with me through Liz's words, I believe you'll come face-to-face with your reflection being Christ Himself; Jesus saying to you, "We are now one flesh".

The mystery of this new, sacred, Divine union unveiled (Eph 5:28-32). As you behold your daring new reflection and become animated by His life through you, His character and nature will become your thoughts, your ways, and new light-filled personality.

My family-friendship and ministry partnership with Liz and her husband, Wesley, have given me the privileged opportunity to witness their immersion in the radiance of God living through humanity. It's provoking and been the greatest encouragement to me and everyone I'm acquainted with who also knows them; that we too are also called to be His Bride, risen and resplendent, victorious and even more importantly, each called by Him, "His Beloved".

Ben Dianda
Founder, Magnify

My relationship with Liz began a few years ago. The moment I met her, I knew her to be a rare find. As I have grown in relationship with her, I find her to be a modern Madame Guyon. Her deep connection and love for God is heart melting. Her teachings have not only touched my heart but are of unique spiritual potency.

I know such potency to proceed from her personal life of stillness and love exchange with the Bridegroom. I encourage every reader to meditate on each of the short excerpts from Reflecting God and believe that God will increase this in your life.

Eric Gilmour
Founder, Sonship International

FOREWORD

ERIC GILMOUR

J ust before the grey light began to herald the dawn, my daughter and I made our way to the soothing shores to watch the sunrise. Breaking over the edge of the earth, the rays of what can only be likened to glory, silenced us with awe. She, having had her breath taken away from the sight, noticed that we were the only people on the shore.

After a few minutes of this majestic art of the Divine Craftsman, she said to me, "That was such a beautiful experience. You know, it is so sad that no one came out to see it". What an illustration of humanity's greatest tragedy. The Son of God is so beautiful every single day and so few go out to meet Him.

For God, who said, "Light shall shine out of darkness," is the One who has shone in our hearts to give the Light of the knowledge of the glory of God in the face of Christ.
2 Cor 4:6 (NASB)

As Charles Spurgeon has written, "Is there not a charm in His every feature?" and "He will never be anything otherwise than all fair". Jesus

Christ, the face of God, is our universal solution. The lack of the knowing of Him is the darkness in which the world sits.

Our greatest joys are found basking in His beams. It is not common knowledge but nonetheless true, that fruit is insipid (tasteless) without time in the sun. No amount of care or effort can make up for the lack of direct contact with the sun. So are we.

Without His glory lighting upon us we have nothing to fulfil us and therefore nothing to develop us into His Divine image.

Men love to wrestle and fight to gain what they want, but God is far beyond the ability to be manipulated. We are utterly helpless, unable to conform ourselves into the image of Jesus.

For as the Puritans wrote, "If the sun be gone all the candles in the world cannot make it day". But as 2 Corinthians 3:16-18 (ASV) states, whenever a person turns towards the Lord, he becomes one who is *beholding as in a mirror the glory of the Lord* and is being *transformed into the same image from glory to glory.*

Praise Jesus! He does the work! One cannot chip an iceberg into water, but if that iceberg basks in the sun, the rivers will begin to flow. So many are trying to chisel their way into the sweet flow of the Spirit by efforts and striving. They soon fail of fatigue. Yet, if one will come to Jesus, they will find rest and ease (Matthew 11:28).

God has given simplicity in Jesus. All is in One. As A.W. Tozer stated, "a man who has met God is not looking for anything because he has found It".

At the time of this writing the American people are in an uproar. Politics, riots, racism, Marxism, manipulations and a pandemic are upon us. Yet Jesus is just as lovely today as He ever was. He is still brightness extreme and a bleeding dream. I look at the past and see that the beauty of Christ has always lifted those who believe into a bliss above the earth. Even in the crackle of the flame the martyrs sang of His infinite charms.

In conclusion, I want to encourage each reader to lift up God's Holy Son. He is still more than enough and the universal solution to all the problems of mankind.

One summer, as the day died and night took its reign, I lay in a field with my youngest daughter. Staring at the stars she said to me with childlike intrigue, "Daddy, where do the stars go in the daytime?".

Through my smile I said, "Baby, they are always there. It is just that the sun is so high and so bright that you cannot see them anymore". I knew that God was whispering in my ear, "If you lift the Son to the heights He will extinguish all lesser lights. If you take the Son out of the heights you will begin to see all kinds of lesser lights".

How many of us find ourselves tormented with lust, greed, comparison, fear, competition, anger, grief, confusion, etc? He is the solution. Lift Him higher. Silently come before Him and let the stillness of your heart yield up to Him affectionate adoration. The image of the One you are giving attention to will soon gain more and more ground in your life.

There is a daily knowing that comes from a daily stillness.

Psalm 46 shows us that God is exalted in the Nations when we are *still and know that He is God*. This is the importance of sitting still at His feet everyday. When a lake is still, it reflects the image of what is above it.

His,

Eric Gilmour
Founder, Sonship International

"You are the reflection of Jesus on earth now; His living, breathing image"

- Liz Wright

THE INVITATION

...all that Jesus now is, so are we in this world.

1 John 4:17

A life utterly transformed by Christ's Spirit is the most exhilarating, fulfilling, powerful life we can ever imagine. It is God's dream for you to live this way, experiencing the reality of New Creation Life, every day. You are the revelation of Jesus on earth now. His reflection! He wants you to know this as your constant reality, experiencing who you truly are and to shine with His glory.

God is here right now on planet earth; in you! You are His living, breathing image.

Just pause for a moment and consider deeply what you have just read. As this realisation drops from your head to your heart, you will be transported into a whole new reality. As faith ignites within you, you will see that YOU are the victory of the cross!

Jesus longs for you to live this way; feeling His love every moment, experiencing freedom in every area of your life, as one now filled with His Divine nature. He wants your heart wrapped in the comfort of Heaven and overflowing with peace.

Jesus wants your mind infused, accessing unlimited wisdom and creativity, your body overflowing with supernatural energy, with sickness of mind, body and heart a thing of the past because they do not exist within the Person of Christ. He wants you to know the healing power of God dispensing through you, touching every aspect of your life and the lives of everyone you love.

All over the world people are awakening now, knowing there is more and beginning to untangle from beliefs and ways of living that no longer satisfy. It's time for us to rise up and to shine, to live as a reflection of our Creator and to step out of the influence of the old nature completely.

This book will change your life! It is your invitation to go deeper than you've ever imagined possible, into experiencing the bliss and joy of your union with Jesus. It will help escort you into this glorious, awakened life, reconnected to the One who has His arms wide open to welcome you home into His Presence.

I encourage you to spend time in each life-transforming key, staying in each one for several days or weeks if necessary. Keep revisiting the keys through which you feel fresh life and strength coming into you. I invite you to open your heart, to read each one slowly and to let your focus be Jesus!

Listen for His still, small voice whispering His truth to you. Embrace Him. Wrap the arms of your love and attention around Him.

Remember, He is closer than your breath and His promise is to transform you!

Now it's time to be made new by every revelation that's been given to you. And to be transformed as you embrace the glorious Christ-within as your new life and live in union with him!
Eph 4:23-24

You have always been the dream of God. You have value beyond comprehension. Your love for Jesus, no matter how weak or compromised you may feel, is the reward of His sufferings. Your love is what He died for. You are extraordinary. You are safe and you are completely, utterly loved.

Jesus is drawing you deeper into Him. For a few moments every day, find somewhere you can just sit and be still. Shut the world out. Come into the present moment. Let go, and as you read each word, gaze. Have a single focus on the Person of Christ and you will become immersed in God.

"How deep is God's love! He gives Himself to those who have made a place for Him. He becomes their end, their fullness, their everything"

- Madame Jeanne Guyon

TRUE IDENTITY

"You are the inheritance of Jesus, the reward of His sufferings, His resting place on earth now"

E phesians 1:18 is known as one of the famous apostolic prayers. When we study this scripture in Western Aramaic and Hebrew, Paul's words can be understood as a proclamation to us from the heart of Jesus. Through this lens, we see that Paul wasn't asking God to help us 'one day' attain these incredible, spiritual realities but was actually decreeing His intention for us. He was showing us the way of life as a New Creation.

With this in mind, I invite you to read this scripture, receiving it as a proclamation from the heart of Jesus for you to experience from this very moment;

...the light of God will illuminate the eyes of your imagination, flooding you with light, until you experience the full revelation of the hope of his calling—that is, the wealth of God's glorious inheritances that he finds in us, his holy ones!

"Jesus, I thank you that the eyes of my brother or sister's heart are now beginning to flood with light. Thank you that in the depth of their being, they will know their immense value as a New Creation in You. As they look at You, in whose image they have been made, I thank you that their hearts will continually flood with revelation; seeing, feeling and knowing they have value beyond compare because You have chosen them to belong to You and their nature is now Yours.

I thank you, Jesus, for filling their hearts with love, meeting their every need, casting out and melting away all fear, unbelief, low self-esteem and low self-worth. I thank you for removing all false definitions of who they are, and any belief that defines their identity in a way that is contrary to the truth. I thank you for each one's heart flooding with truth. Amen".

I believe Holy Spirit is moving in you right now, beginning to fill you afresh with the experience of His love and showing you how you are seen in Heaven. He is showing you who you truly are and your immense value.

The intention of Jesus' heart, is that you would feel how precious you are to Him and therefore be liberated to walk confidently, empowered by His love and consequently, living in freedom.

Jesus desires that you'd experience His Spirit and love within you as the supernatural source and strength of your life continually. I can feel in my heart as I write this, Him longing for you to take hold of His outstretched hand and step into this shift in your reality.

But the one who joins himself to the Lord is mingled into one spirit with him.
1 Cor 6:17

You are a New Creation made from the very substance of the uncreated God who is resident within you now as your new nature!

I encourage you to stay here for just a few minutes longer. Invite Holy Spirit to continue to flood the eyes of your heart with His light and to meet your every need. Embrace Jesus' Presence within, holding Him with your heart's gaze. Remember, it's as we embrace Christ-within that we are transformed by every unfolding revelation and this is your moment.

Now it's time to be made new by every revelation that's been given to you. And to be transformed as you embrace the glorious Christ-within as your new life and live in union with him!
Eph 4:23-24

Slowly read this scripture again over and over. The words are intended to escort you through the doorway they provide, until you are fully immersed in God's Presence and completely enveloped by His love.

...God will illuminate the eyes of your imagination, flooding you with light, until you experience the full revelation of the hope of his calling—that is, the wealth of God's glorious inheritances that he finds in us, his holy ones!
Eph 1:18

This is your new life and Jesus wants you fully aligned into the experience of it. It is a life designed to abound in grace and to overflow in fruitfulness. You are the inheritance of Jesus, the reward of His sufferings, His resting place on earth now. Secure in Father's love, you are forever changed in your nature.

Living within you is the Christ who floods you with the expectation of glory!
Col 1:27

JOURNAL

As you read this chapter, what truths about your identity did Jesus stir in your spirit? I encourage you to write them down and meditate upon them. You can even speak them as declarations over yourself daily. This is a powerful exercise to dismantle false constructs of your identity!

THE FAITH OF JESUS

"It is Christ's faith that enables your supernatural capacity to believe in Him and therefore to live at rest in Him"

E phesians 1:19 says, *I pray that you will continually experience the immeasurable greatness of God's power made available to you through faith. Then your lives will be an advertisement of this immense power as it works through you!* This is God's intention for your life, that you will continually experience the immeasurable greatness of His power made available to you through faith; through the gift of faith that Christ has released to you.

And now the essence of this new life is no longer mine, for the Anointed One lives his life through me—we live in union as one! My new life is empowered by the faith of the Son of God who loves me so much that he gave himself for me, and dispenses his life into mine!
Gal 2:20

It is Christ's faith that enables your supernatural capacity to believe in Him and therefore to live at rest in Him. This gift enables you to experience the immeasurable greatness of God's power continually.

Paul continues, His intention is that your life would consequently *be an advertisement of this immense power as it works through you!* As you experience the Living God inside of you, Christ then radiates out of you. Through you, Jesus continues His ministry of healing the sick, raising the dead, cleansing the lepers, casting out the demonic, restoring everything in this realm to His original design.

The same one who descended is also the one who ascended above the heights of heaven, in order to begin the restoration and fulfillment of all things.

Eph 4:10

As Jesus continues His ministry through us, we are going to see the life of Christ increasing everywhere we go. The very Presence of God drips from our lives as we choose to stay in communion with Him. All He wants us to do is to sit down on the inside and enjoy our union with Him. He will do the rest as we simply lean into Him.

Yet how much more radiant is this new and glorious ministry of the Spirit that shines from us!

2 Cor 3:8

I invite you to begin to thank Holy Spirit for His indwelling Presence and as you do, to notice how the supernatural faith of Jesus gently and powerfully begins to reignite within you. The moment you feel His Presence, stay there. Allow His love to pour through you as a healing balm, enveloping and soothing you.

Drink in again the strength contained within Galatians 2:20. Keep your heart's attention fixed on Jesus as you read. The same faith we see demonstrated in the life of Christ as He lived among us, is the faith that resides within you now! Faith is a Person!

And now the essence of this new life is no longer mine, for the Anointed One lives his life through me—we live in union as one! My new life is empowered by the faith of the Son of God who loves me so much that he gave himself for me, and dispenses his life into mine!

As Jesus dispenses fresh faith into you, He is reframing your reality and breaking you free from false constructs that are made up of the beliefs that the world and its systems offer. He is infusing you with truth and power.

Just linger, savouring this holy moment, valuing and honouring His Presence. As you do this, you will be enfolded by God and will enter more deeply into true, internal rest. The world and its cares will grow dim and you will find Jesus beginning to share His heart's desires with you. This is all fruit of the *immeasurable greatness of God's power* that's now made available to us through the faith of Jesus. This is the interior life.

...because as he is, so also are we, in this world.
1 John 4:17 (ABPE)

We are alive now in Christ. His immeasurable power brings forth supernatural life and faith inside of us; the capacity to believe Him, to live in rest, to lie on the chest of Jesus. Here you can rest in the boat of your life during the storm, enfolded in the arms of Grace, in the arms of the One who collapses chaos and overrules all the activity of darkness.

As we prioritise our relationship this way, we begin to see His immeasurable greatness continuing to manifest within us and then through us, to calm the storms of life everywhere we go. We are the ones, who now in Christ, have been pre-destined to rule the atmosphere of our world. This is the co-reigning life of the Bride; fully one, fully leaning.

This is His intended way of life for you in every moment; it is the New Creation life that is now yours in Jesus. As we learn to live in His strength and with Heaven's perspective undergirding us, our heart motive becomes purified, desiring only to love and reflect God. We begin to emerge as Shining Ones.

JOURNAL

Are there any areas that Jesus is inviting you to entrust to Him today, so you can stay surrendered in rest and confident in His immense power working through you?

What would it look like for you to continually experience the *immeasurable greatness of His power*? What would be different in your life if you remained at rest and trusted His faith to be at work within you? Meditate on this, for it is your new nature and your true reality!

EVERY NEED SATISFIED

"Jesus wants you knowing that every single weakness, every single challenge, every single difficulty in your life, will all be met by Him"

Philippians 4:19 says, *I am convinced that my God will fully satisfy every need you have, for I have seen the abundant riches of glory revealed to me through the Anointed One, Jesus Christ!* As I began to look at this scripture for you today, I saw Jesus, in the spirit, wrapping His arms around you. I saw Him taking you into His embrace, pulling you to His chest, enabling you to lean into His strength.

I felt His desire to pour fresh peace into you, the peace that calms any emotional storm going on inside of you, and soothes away all pain, grief, insecurity and fear. Let's read this scripture again slowly. This is Jesus' intention for you. Listen with your spirit. I encourage you to open your heart to feel His love, to hear Holy Spirit speaking directly to you as you read.

I am convinced that my God will fully satisfy every need you have, for I have seen the abundant riches of glory revealed to me through the Anointed One, Jesus Christ!

Jesus' desire is for every single need you have in the circumstances of your life and in your heart, to be fully satisfied by Him. If you have sickness in your body, any struggles in your mind, any form of torment or depression, anything; He wants to heal it all.

Jesus wants you to understand who you are in Him and who you are to Him. He wants you to have Heaven's perspective regarding how He's redeeming the circumstances of your life. He wants your heart resting and confident, with completely immovable faith that's empowered by Him, certain that He is for you.

Jesus wants you knowing that every single weakness, every single challenge, every single difficulty in your life, will all be met by Him. He will be glorified in your life and will increase His testimony through what He does in turning every situation around for good.

Everything we see recorded in the Gospels is how Jesus is. He is the same yesterday, today and forever. He healed the sick. He raised the dead. He cleansed the lepers. He cast out demons. That is what He does! As the Divine touches the natural, it transforms, coming out from darkness and its bondage to decay. He is your Redeemer. He is your Saviour. He is your Healer and He is your King.

Jesus is healing your heart right now, showing you how safe and loved you really are. He's showing you His desire to meet your every need, that He is for you and is within you. He is releasing to you the faith and grace to know Him in His sovereignty!

And never forget that I am with you every day, even to the completion
of this age!

\- Jesus

Matt 28:20

JOURNAL

Write down the needs that come to mind: your physical, emotional, mental, relational and spiritual needs.

All that you have just written down is actually Jesus' list. No longer consider this *your* list, but *His*! This isn't a list of lack or things unfulfilled in your life, it is actually a list of expectancy because He is the One who is going to fulfil every one of these things! You can celebrate in thankfulness and be at rest, knowing that He is your Source and Provider.

How would it feel to completely trust Jesus to meet all of your needs? Meditate on the peace and rest it brings into your heart and sit in thankfulness before Him.

HIS PERFECT PLAN

"He will accomplish everything that has been predestined for you, for He is God and you are His Beloved!"

P aul says in Romans 8:28, *So we are convinced that every detail of our lives is continually woven together to fit into God's perfect plan of bringing good into our lives, for we are his lovers who have been called to fulfill his designed purpose.* The word 'meditation' means to have a single focus. With this in mind, let's read this verse again slowly, being fully present.

Let yourself feel the meaning and implication of each word. As your mind focuses, allow your heart to engage with Jesus. Feel His love flowing through this profound insight into the ways of God. Notice the hope beginning to rise within you.

So we are convinced that every detail of our lives is continually woven together to fit into God's perfect plan of bringing good into our lives, for we are his lovers who have been called to fulfill his designed purpose.

What is He saying to you? As His Spirit and Word begin releasing fresh life and empowerment into you, expect a new measure of security in His sovereignty to awaken within your heart. In this moment, you are experiencing absolute truth!

No matter how you feel, no matter how out of control things might seem to be in your world, the intention of Jesus' heart is clear; every single detail of your life is *continually woven together to fit into God's perfect plan* to bring goodness into your life.

So if you can't make sense of things right now, I encourage you to take a moment longer and lean into His Presence, into this truth and into the faithfulness of who Jesus is. Savour these words. Read them slowly over and over until you feel joy beginning to bubble up from deep within your spirit. Listen to His heart. He is speaking to you. He is drawing you into an encounter with His love.

So we are convinced that every detail of our lives is continually woven together to fit into God's perfect plan of bringing good into our lives, for we are his lovers who have been called to fulfill his designed purpose.
Rom 8:28

Let go of your circumstances. Release each burden and impossibility into His capable hands. Sink back into the arms of Grace. He is here for you. You are enfolded in His Presence. Let the eyes of your spirit search out the expression of Jesus' face, for they allow revelation-light to flood your soul.

Remember His nature: He is love, He is kindness, He is your wise, protective, tender, sovereign King. Every single detail of your life is being *continually woven together* right now, worked into conformity with the counsel of His perfect will.

This is God's work in our lives as His Spirit resides within us and Heaven is mobilized on our behalf. Jesus is establishing all things, bringing you forth completely filled with Him, perfected as the reflection of God in the earth. Decree this truth over yourself while looking into your eyes in a mirror, as you do, see Him looking back at you;

"I am the revelation of You, Jesus! Your beautiful Presence is within me, filling my eyes with glistening light. Every detail of my life is Your story".

There is nothing outside of Jesus' redemptive power. Your life is under His supreme headship. He is the Alpha and the Omega. He is the One who wraps up human history according to His desires and plans that were decided before the foundation of the earth. He will accomplish everything that has been predestined for you, for He is God and you are His Beloved!

"Jesus, I thank you for Your Spirit dispensing fresh power and faith within the heart of my precious brother or sister to see and believe again. I thank you for Your truth igniting deep within their heart. Thank you for Your grace that's releasing a secure and immovable trust which enables them to rest in the truth that You're working all things together for their good.

You are bringing forth Your perfect plan in their life. Their entire life is continually bathed in Your redeeming, transforming power because You are present within them. Amen".

I bless you to rest in the midst of whatever storm is going on in your life, supernaturally trusting in Jesus' faithfulness. I celebrate with you, as each one begins to subside and as victory is brought out of each challenge or tragedy you face. I bless you with deep and complete rest, for He is faithful.

JOURNAL

Write down the situations in your life that you've already seen God redeem and use for your good. Meditate on these testimonies and ask Holy Spirit to reveal even more deeply, how completely He has used those things for good. Let Him show you the depths of how victoriously He has redeemed those circumstances. Let thankfulness rise within you as you meditate on His goodness.

Now, with your heart full of gratitude and faith, bring the situations you haven't yet seen used for good. Let hope arise within you and trust that the story isn't over! Let your spirit and soul dwell in thankfulness through faith. Praise Him for the redemption you have not yet seen, knowing that He will work these things for good as well.

I encourage you to share the testimonies you've meditated on today. It's a powerful practice to testify about the goodness of God, as it strengthens your own faith and also encourages others!

GAINING HEAVEN'S PERSPECTIVE

"We were created to live completely secure, radiating every attribute of His nature as our own"

A s you enter in through today's key, I encourage you to begin to thank Jesus for a fresh ability and sensitivity to hear, believe and receive the intention of His heart for you. What you are about to read is your true reality, beyond the temporal circumstances that you face right now. This scripture reveals who we are, what this journey is all about and how history will ultimately conclude.

As you read this scripture, fresh grace will be dispensed through you and will attune your spiritual senses. I know your life will change because we are transformed by every unfolding revelation.

Day by day, as you step through the doorway of the Living Word, you are entering into the realm of Jesus' Presence where you access the powerful vantage point of Divine perspective. This is where we begin to understand and experience Jesus' supreme authority.

My passion is to enlighten every person to this divine mystery. It was hidden from ages past until now, and kept a secret in the heart of God, the Creator of all. The purpose of this was to unveil before every throne and rank of angelic orders of the heavenly realm God's full and diverse wisdom revealed through the church.

Eph 3:9-10

That's You! You are what the angels are observing. They are filled with awe and wonder as Christ, the Master Potter, perfects His living, breathing image. YOU were predestined to reveal the manifold wisdom, beauty, holiness and power of God.

This is who we are: light beings, shining ones. We were created to be completely filled with God, able to experience His love in every moment as we're continually strengthened by the power of His Spirit in our inner man. We were created to live completely secure, radiating every attribute of His nature as our own.

I encourage you to read this scripture again slowly, taking in the truth that Jesus passionately wants you to understand, not just intellectually but with all of your heart. He wants you impacted by the magnificence of His unfolding plan and to take you into the exquisite experience of all He has done. You are and will forever be a partaker of the Divine nature! This is irreversible. You are the victory of the cross!

My passion is to enlighten every person to this divine mystery. It was hidden from ages past until now, and kept a secret in the heart of God, the Creator of all. The purpose of this was to unveil before every throne and rank of angelic orders of the heavenly realm God's full and diverse wisdom revealed through the church.
Eph 3:9-10

I bless you today, that your heart and spirit would arise and soar. I bless you to be completely caught up on the inside with this extraordinary truth and be transformed in your inner stature. It's time!

Everything obscuring your vision and hindering your ability to experience Jesus' immense love for you is being removed. I decree breakthrough over you! I decree the intention of Jesus' heart for you to move into a totally different place right now.

He wants you filled with confidence, fully awake on the inside, walking powerfully, strong and free as His beloved New Creation. I bless you to be aware, with all of your heart, that You are the masterpiece of God, unveiled before the angelic orders of the Heavenly realms.

Never doubt God's mighty power to work in you and accomplish all this. He will achieve infinitely more than your greatest request, your most unbelievable dream, and exceed your wildest imagination! He will outdo them all, for His miraculous power constantly energizes you.

Eph 3:20

JOURNAL

Visualise Jesus standing in the middle of any troubling circumstance in your life. Picture yourself stepping into Him as He stands in the midst of that situation that is on your heart. You are one with Him, so begin to look through His eyes and let Him flood you with His perspective and manifold wisdom.

What does it feel like to be filled with His Divine nature as you look at this situation? Write what it looks like now as you stand victoriously in Him, looking from His view and filled with the power of His nature.

ENFOLDED INTO CHRIST

"Sitting down on the inside in God-consciousness and reflecting and releasing the King, enables us to co-reign by simply being who we are!"

In 2 Corinthians 5:17, Paul says, *Now, if anyone is enfolded into Christ, he has become an entirely new person. All that is related to the old order has vanished. Behold, everything is fresh and new.* We're going to read this astounding truth again, personalising each word and making sure you are fully present.

Shut out every distraction. Let your heart lock onto Jesus. Wrap the arms of your heart around His indwelling Spirit. Breathe out the cares of your life. Yawn, stretch, relax. As you do, let go of every situation you face.

This is your moment. Jesus is waiting with arms wide open. He longs for your heart to open towards Him and for you to feel Him enfolding you. Dare to allow Him to undo you with His love and to lift out all pain as He infuses you with peace.

As you slowly and intentionally read each word, over and over if necessary, notice and pause when Holy Spirit begins to flow in your heart. In these moments, God's life is beginning to gently surge through you, resurrecting and filling you. As you read, let the Living Word carry you into a fresh encounter.

Now, [I am] *enfolded into Christ.* [I have] *become an entirely new person. All that is related to the old order has vanished.* [I can see] *everything is fresh and new.*

1 Cor 5:17 [text added]

You in Christ and Christ in you; intertwined, inseparable, one being. There is no power in any dimension of creation, nor within the realm of eternity, that's able to override God's decision to dwell in you. Nothing can separate you from Jesus. You can relax and simply enjoy Him, trusting in His enfolding.

The enemy attacks us by trying to desensitise us from this reality. He understands that the more secure we are in Christ, the more we're able to internally rest in His Presence, the more we're convinced of the New Creation reality and the more we're able to live centred in this experience; then the more power radiates effortlessly from our lives.

Sitting down on the inside in God-consciousness and reflecting and releasing the King, enables us to co-reign by simply being who we are!

We have stepped into the time where each one of us will begin to co-reign, not intermittently but continually and effortlessly. We will live powerfully and free, centred in Christ, experiencing the truth that we are seated with Him in Heavenly places. We will no longer go in and out; sometimes feeling connected, sometimes feeling far away from His Presence, depending on the emotional state we're in.

We will now live with our spirits in ascendancy, experiencing Jesus as the core strength of our lives.

I bless you with being completely connected to this reality. You are upheld by the very power of the uncreated God. He is the substance of your being now. You are an entirely new species. You are a new creation and part of the new order of things. God is upholding all of it so you can rest and be confident, enjoying your relationship with Jesus.

The Truth has set you free! He is closer than your breath. We have been restored to pristine innocence. All things have been made new. Stay in this moment. His Presence and truth are transforming you!

JOURNAL

Can you recall times when you experienced His indwelling Presence so strongly that His nature was flowing through you with ease? What was different about your life?

Ask Holy Spirit to help you surrender anything that causes you to step into your own strength. Let Him fill you with His stability. What would be transformed in your life if you remained consistently living out of His nature

THE DIVINE EMBRACE

"Jesus is simplifying your walk, bringing you back into His embrace
and the experience of His love"

A s you take hold of this powerful scripture, it will literally change your life. This revelation Holy Spirit unfolds for us through the apostle Paul is the secret. It is the access key to New Creation living. This is *how* we live life in the Spirit. He presents before us what has happened to us, why it has happened and how we are to maintain this wondrous way of life.

As you see this today and step through the doorway of His Living Word, you will experience a greater degree of fullness and enjoyment in your relationship with Jesus. Your entire life will transform! I encourage you to read every word slowly and as you do, begin to *do* the Word and step in.

*...be transformed as you embrace the glorious Christ-within and live
in union with him!*
Eph 4:24

You are transformed by simply embracing Jesus' Presence within you and choosing to live this moment in the beautiful union you're invited to enjoy.

He is opening the eyes of your understanding right now. He is empowering you to experience the reality of your union with Him like never before. He is untangling you from every remaining trace of religious striving and fear-driven living, even from struggling in your own strength to keep believing.

Jesus is simplifying your walk, bringing you back into His embrace and the experience of His love. Your life can now become an unfolding walk of intimacy with God, transformed by every unfolding revelation that He pours into your heart.

The second half of Ephesians 4:24 says, *For God has re-created you all over again in his perfect righteousness, and you now belong to him in the realm of true holiness.* The NIV translation reads, *created to be like God in true righteousness and holiness.*

As you stay with Jesus for just a few minutes longer, wrap the arms of your honour and thankfulness around Him. In humility, accept all He's said to you as the truth. What He's done for us is utterly phenomenal. Who He has recreated us to be is unfathomable; ones *like God in true righteousness and holiness,* His beloved mirror-image, the very revelation of Almighty God on earth!

Embracing the indwelling Christ and being with Him is the wisest thing we'll ever do.

This is your life now, to be intoxicated and transformed by Divine love and having your every need satisfied. This is our life in Him. Like the Shulamite in Song of Songs 2:5 we too can say we are lovesick for our Beloved!

"We are overwhelmed by your immense love, Jesus. In this moment, we give you all that we are again. We give you every tiny movement of our weak but willing hearts. We are undone!"

JOURNAL

Meditate on the reality that Christ is IN you, that He isn't distant but within your very being! What would transform in your life if you lived in this awareness constantly?

Ask Jesus how He feels about you and write down what He shares with you. If you ever feel yourself wobble, return to this love letter and read it over and over. Let His words affirm you as you embrace the glorious Christ within.

THE COMFORT OF HEAVEN

"His blueprint for your life is to live as one wrapped in the comfort of His great love for you and to know Heaven as your home"

Colossians 2:2 holds another major, life-altering key. Filled with God's love and intention for every believer, Paul lays before us the way we are to live. Take a moment before you read this extraordinary truth to prepare your heart to receive. Begin to breathe in the essence of His Spirit.

Focus the eyes of your heart onto Jesus within you. Thank Him for His indwelling Presence and come fully into this moment. As you thank Jesus for being within you, you will find Him gently flooding you with fresh wisdom, infusing you with Divine knowledge and re-sensitising you to the realm you now live in; the Kingdom within!

As you enter into a place of inner stillness, continue to gaze on Him. You are entering into face-to-face communion.

I can feel in my spirit as I'm writing this, that Holy Spirit is releasing an increase of supernatural sensitivity, opening the eyes of your understanding and giving you the grace you need to behold the Lamb. Jesus is about to share His heart with you and what matters to Him. He is going to take you deeper.

Read this profound promise slowly, let your heart digest each word's meaning. Feel God's heart intention for you in Paul's prayer. Say "Yes" as light enters your heart. Receive and step in.

I am contending for you that your hearts will be wrapped in the comfort of heaven and woven together into love's fabric. This will give you access to all the riches of God as you experience the revelation of God's great mystery—Christ.

Col 2:2

Now let's declare this scripture as a decree from your heart to the heart of Jesus:

[My heart] *will be wrapped in the comfort of heaven and woven together into love's fabric. This will give* [me] *access to all the riches of God* [as I] *experience the revelation of God's great mystery—Christ.*

Col 2:2 [text added]

Holy Spirit wants you to thrive in life, living in the fullness of all that Jesus died to provide. His blueprint for your life is to live as one wrapped in the comfort of His great love for you and to know Heaven as your home. He intends for you to be completely secure and at rest as you live in the continual experience of Christ within you.

Jesus longs for you to understand that as you experience Him within you and are wrapped in the comfort of this profound experience, this extraordinary way of life gives you access to all the riches of God. Right now, Jesus is bringing you into such a place of comfort and security, confident in His absolute faithfulness, strengthened by His love, enjoying Him above all else and co-reigning with Him. He desires for you to be His resting place.

Stay in this place with Jesus for a little longer. Treasure this moment, for it is holy. The God of the universe is wrapping you in His arms and transforming your life. He is awakening you into the life experience He always planned for you to know.

JOURNAL

In what areas of your heart have you received His comfort before? In those experiences, what riches or treasures did you receive from Him?

Are there any places in your heart right now that need to receive comfort? Take some time to open your heart to Him and let His comfort and love wrap around you. Feel Him protect your vulnerability, for He is safe and He is good.

SATAN HAS NO CLAIM

"All that is not of Jesus and His Kingdom will detach from our lives and the lives of those we love as we release His governmental Presence"

I n John 14:30 (AMPCE) Jesus says of Satan, *And he has no claim on Me. [He has nothing in common with Me; there is nothing in Me that belongs to him, and he has no power over Me.]* Jesus is the firstborn among us. He is the prototype of the New Creation. As we look at Jesus, His life becomes a mirror, revealing to us who we are now and our new way of life in Him.

His Presence within invites us to go beyond mere observation and to enter into a continual state of God-consciousness. Jesus intends for us to experience oneness with His mind and heart in every moment.

As you slowly read this extraordinary scripture again, meditate on the fact that this same Jesus that Satan has no power over, is present within you right now. He's not a separate entity but is one with you; inseparable. One nature! He is the very source and strength of your life.

And he has no claim on Me. [He has nothing in common with Me; there is nothing in Me that belongs to him, and he has no power over Me.]

Jesus is flooding the eyes of your heart with fresh light, enabling you to see that Satan's only weapon against you is deception. As a New

Creation in Christ, filled with God's beautiful, radiant, powerful Spirit, Satan has no power over you!

My old identity has been co-crucified with Messiah and no longer lives; for the nails of his cross crucified me with him. And now the essence of this new life is no longer mine, for the Anointed One lives his life through me—we live in union as one! My new life is empowered by the faith of the Son of God who loves me so much that he gave himself for me, and dispenses his life into mine!
Gal 2:20

There is no sin in Jesus. There's no sickness in Jesus. There are no demons in Jesus. There's nothing from the realm of darkness that is in Christ. As we invite His Spirit within to saturate us, consume us and surround us, everything from the realm of darkness detaches from our lives.

As we choose to abide and step out from the old way of life, we prioritise His nature as our source of life and strength. This new nature we express through our words, prayers and conduct will increasingly crush Satan under our feet because the revelation of Jesus flows through us.

All that is not of Jesus and His Kingdom will detach from our lives and the lives of those we love as we release His governmental Presence. In the spirit, I can see Jesus taking hold of your hand and leading you out from all that has held you captive and into a spacious place. I can see you with your arms outstretched above you, breathing in the fresh, pure air of freedom, filled with joy.

Read the following statement slowly and intentionally. As you speak every word, let your heart overflow with thankfulness to Jesus for all He has done for you. Tell Him how you want to live as the full expression of all He accomplished at the cross. Thank Him that you are His living image, pre-destined to reflect everything He purposed in His heart for you as His beloved Bride!

"Satan has no claim on me for I am a new creation in Christ. He has nothing in common with me because of my new nature. There is nothing in me that belongs to him because everything within me now is Christ. It's no longer I but Christ who lives in me. Jesus is my life, therefore nothing in me belongs to the enemy and so he has no power over me!".

Today I decree that you will step into the experience of knowing with all your heart, the victorious position that you sit in right now. YOU are the victory of the cross! I decree you will have the Lord's perspective regarding your life, about how secure you are and who you are. I decree you will see the power that's available to you, in every moment, to overcome every situation!

I decree that you reign supreme over every challenge you face, as you draw on and release the life of Jesus within you. I decree that a renewed faith will ignite within you, releasing the supernatural grace to overcome as your heart is strengthened by the irreversible truth that

Satan has no power over you. You have been set free by the Son of God. He resides within you and so you are free indeed!

JOURNAL

Write down the circumstances that you want to take authority over today. Picture Jesus high above in Heavenly places, seated on the throne. That is where you are as well! This is your true reality. You are seated in Him. From this place, look over those situations and see them through Jesus' eyes.

What are the areas within yourself that you want to align with the truth that Satan has no claim and it's no longer you who lives but Christ? What would victory look like in those areas?

ALL THINGS RESTORED

"As you co-reign in the sweetness and power of your restored union, Jesus will unfold even more of who He is through your life, and the absolutely immovable victory of the cross!"

In 1 Corinthians 15:45-49 Paul says; *For it is written: The first man, Adam, became a living soul. The last Adam became the life-giving Spirit. However, the spiritual didn't come first. The natural precedes the spiritual. The first man was from the dust of the earth; the second Man is the Lord Jehovah, from the realm of heaven.*

The first one, made from dust, has a race of people just like him, who are also made from dust. The One sent from heaven has a race of heavenly people who are just like him. Once we carried the likeness of the man of dust, but now let us carry the likeness of the Man of heaven.

Savour these precious words for a moment and let your heart take in their impact. The truth of what happened at the cross is your core strength. Focus the eyes of your spirit onto Jesus, allowing fresh, revelation-light to enter your whole being. Feel the tender yet fiercely passionate love that compelled Him.

As Jesus looked into the future He saw you; His own reflection! He knew that one day you would look at Him with eyes full of love. This was the hope that strengthened Him, His desire for this moment with you!

With Golgotha's final, conclusive blow, Love became evident as the strongest force. The work of redemption for His beloved Adam (and each member of this precious, fallen race) became irreversible and untouchable. Jesus, fully God and fully man, had overcome. As the eyes of your heart open to this profound truth, you also will overcome in every way!

All that was stolen from Adam and Father at the Fall was restored by Jesus at the cross. He has restored the joy and wonder of uninterrupted, face-to-face friendship, the exhilarating partnership that Adam and Father shared, of Creator and beloved stewarding, protecting and developing creation together.

Remember, this same Jesus, the King of Glory, resides within you. He desires for you to experience His love and for all things to be restored in your life. As a precious member of this extraordinary New Creation, you have complete authority over the realm of darkness. You too can once again steward, protect and co-create, not only in your life but this earth, to see everything come back into its pre-Fall state!

Your life now is one of co-reigning. This is who you are. This is the supernatural overflow from within you! Your oneness with Jesus has made you fruitful. The enemy was disarmed at the cross. The realm of darkness and its tyrannical tirade was defeated.

I encourage you to stay in this moment for just a little longer. Keep letting go of every pressure as you breathe in and sink deeper into His beautiful Presence that indwells and surrounds you. Listen for Jesus' perspective regarding any situation that remains in bondage in your life. He will give you His mind on the matter.

As you co-reign in the sweetness and power of your restored union, Jesus will unfold even more of who He is through your life, and the absolutely immovable victory of the cross!

JOURNAL

What things are you passionate about seeing restored on the earth? Ask Holy Spirit for decrees you can speak over those people, groups, nations, institutions, businesses or industries.

What parts of your own life have you seen restored by Him? Let gratitude rise in you, along with faith. Present to Him anything that you're still waiting to see restored, full of thankfulness and confidence.

EXPERIENCING A SUPERNATURALLY FULFILLED LIFE

"His life within you is your true nature and strength. This is how we live a truly supernatural life"

T ake a moment before you read the following scriptures to get comfortable and prepare your heart. Set your gaze on Jesus. Breathe in and out deeply and slowly and as you do, let go of all that has jostled for your attention. Imagine every situation slipping gently off your lap as you sit back and sink into the arms of Jesus as His Presence enfolds you. Enter into rest.

This time has been Divinely orchestrated to captivate and reinvigorate your heart. This is your moment. The Beatitudes which you are about to read, contain the power to completely transform how you live. The invitation they carry opens up the way to experience true bliss and prosperity of heart.

Each verse can be experienced. Every word is alive and active, carrying within it God's intention for your life with Him and is therefore transformational in nature. Listen for His promises.

The experience waiting for you as you enter into each attitude of heart will provide you with the richest, most fulfilling life because these are the ways of God. These verses are to be the culture of your marriage-union with Jesus. Welcome to the next chapter of your blessed, supernatural life!

What wealth is offered to you when you feel your spiritual poverty! For there is no charge to enter the realm of heaven's kingdom.

What delight comes to you when you wait upon the Lord! For you will find what you long for.

What blessing comes to you when gentleness lives in you! For you will inherit the earth.

How enriched you are when you crave righteousness! For you will be surrounded with fruitfulness.

How satisfied you are when you demonstrate tender mercy! For tender mercy will be demonstrated to you.

What bliss you experience when your heart is pure! For then your eyes will open to see more and more of God.

How blessed you are when you make peace! For then you will be recognized as a true child of God.

How enriched you are when you bear the wounds of being persecuted for doing what is right! For that is when you experience the realm of heaven's kingdom.

How ecstatic you can be when people insult and persecute you and speak all kinds of cruel lies about you because of your love for me! So leap for joy—since your heavenly reward is great. For you are being rejected the same way the prophets were before you.

Matt 5:3-12

I encourage you to read each line again, this time inviting Jesus to pour into you the attributes of His nature that you need from Him: the gentleness, kindness, compassion or purity of heart that you need. It's in these moments that we shine and become filled again with the supernatural nature of God. It's from this place we begin to live in His promises.

This is how we overcome every challenge in our lives, how we shift atmospheres, how the sick get healed, how the blind eyes open, this is how (as Jesus says in verse 14) *your lives light up the world*. So this is your moment to transform, to step in and allow Jesus' nature to envelop you. His life within you is your true nature and strength. This is how we live a truly supernatural life.

As you live in union with me as your source, fruitfulness will stream from within you.
John 15:5

JOURNAL

As you read the Beatitudes, which verse/s impacted you the most? What does Holy Spirit want to reveal to you?

ACCESSING THE GLORY

"Everything we see Him do is the life we can live, as God resident within us continues to express His life through us"

As I write this key, I can feel Jesus longing to be with you. I can feel Him drawing you into Himself to see Him in His glory. Before you begin to read, I encourage you to get comfortable, breathe deeply and refocus the attention of your heart onto Jesus.

Allow yourself to decompress. Sink deeper and deeper into God's indwelling Presence as you hand over each pressure and every single fear. By entering into this precious moment through the intention of your heart's gaze, you are stepping into the Holy of Holies. This moment contains the experience of your union with Jesus and so is filled with life-transforming power.

From here, everything changes. The pressures and fears you face will begin to dissolve as you see who Jesus is with fresh eyes, and Holy Spirit re-sensitises your capacity to enjoy Him. Let faith and excitement rise within your heart. You are now positioned to experience more of God.

I can see Jesus within you, standing as the doorway, your access point into the realm of Glory. In my spirit, I feel Jesus speaking the same powerful words to you that He spoke to the apostle John:

Don't yield to fear. I am the Beginning and I am the End, the Living One! I was dead, but now look—I am alive forever and ever. And I hold the keys that unlock death and the unseen world.

Rev 1:17-18

When Jesus takes Peter, James and John up the mountain to pray in Luke 9, we are given a further glimpse into who Jesus really is, as the God of the universe unfolds from within Him and for a brief moment, Heaven becomes visible.

As he prayed, his face began to glow until it was a blinding glory streaming from him. His entire body was illuminated with a radiant glory. His brightness became so intense that it made his clothing blinding white, like multiple flashes of lightning. All at once, two men appeared in glorious splendour: Moses and Elijah. They spoke with Jesus about his soon departure from this world and the things he was destined to accomplish in Jerusalem.

Luke 9:29-30

Just as with Peter, James and John, Jesus wants you to experience His glory. He wants you to know, with every fibre of your being, that He is King of kings and Lord of lords. As this transforming revelation moves into your heart, every fear within you will begin to melt like wax.

You'll notice in verse 29, scripture records for us a simple yet incredible key that enables us to continually live in the transforming light of God's glory. It simply says, *As he prayed, his face began to glow.*

When we study the original language of the scriptures, the word translated as 'prayer' carries rich meaning. At its core, it describes a deep, heart-to-heart union and communal bonding, a oneness that provides a deep intimacy where one heart is fully known by the other. As Jesus communed this way with His Father, His face began to glow until there was a blinding glory streaming from Him.

I encourage you to stay here for a moment and savour these words. Remember, Jesus is the firstborn among us; the original of our new species! He is the Way. Everything we see Him do is the life we can live, as God resident within us continues to express His life through us.

A few verses later, we find Jesus back down the mountain delivering a precious boy from fierce, demonic oppression as He shone with the glory-light of who He truly is. This same Shining One lives in you!

I tell you the truth, anyone who believes in me will do the same works I have done, and even greater works, because I am going to be with the Father.
John 14:12 (NLT)

Using some of the language provided for us in Luke 9, let's go even deeper and commune heart-to-heart with Jesus, saying "Yes" to His invitation to see Him in His glory and to be freshly immersed in the transforming light of His Presence;

"Jesus, as You prayed Your face began to glow until it was a blinding glory streaming from You. Your entire body was illuminated with radiance. Your brightness became so intense that it made Your clothing blinding white like flashes of lightning. Jesus, I say 'Yes' to Your invitation to know You this way and see You in Your glory.

Release Your light! Radiate out from the centre of my spirit, as I yield to You as my one true, supreme, majestic God! Immerse me, enfold me, open my eyes to behold You! Transform my perspective. Let me see all of life through the lens of Your sovereignty. I say 'Yes'. Like John, I long to know You in Your resurrection. I trust You and You alone as my source of life.

I am Your reflection and as Your Bride, I choose only You. I let go of all fear, all offence and every attitude of heart that does not reflect Yours. I step out from all dependency on any source of strength other than You. I give You my heart fully and completely. Let all that I am become submerged in You. Be enthroned in every area of my life. Consume me.

Let Your glory radiate through me as Your doorway into the earth, to bathe everyone and every situation I face with Your love and miracle-working power! I choose to commune as I sit in this holy place within Your Presence. Like You, I want to shine with the light of glory that drips Your power, to see every situation completely transformed. Amen".

JOURNAL

What fears, concerns or pressures is Jesus inviting you to surrender today? You are a doorway into the earth, visualise what it will look like in those situations for you to be shining with the light of His glory. Let Jesus fill you with His perspective and ask what He wants to be for you and through you in those areas.

THE IMPACT OF FORGIVENESS

"He longs for each one to experience New Creation Life, which is accessed through the powerful doorway of forgiveness"

I n John 20:19-23, we find Jesus risen from the grave and talking with His beloved disciples. I can only imagine how they must have felt as they looked intently into the face of their Friend, who only days before had died in agony on the cross before their very eyes.

They must have been utterly overwhelmed, each one's emotions swirling with ecstatic joy, incomprehensible relief and awe, as a million fragmented experiences suddenly fit together in one glorious symphony of revelation.

Their beloved Friend was present among them again, only this time, as their resurrected King of Glory. They were free! He was alive! Jesus had secured victory, forever defeating all that separated them from Him: sin, sickness, death and all of darkness' deceptive reign. It was over. Finished.

Everything Jesus had taught them and had been to them, it was all true. The old order of things had passed away. They had been brought into a whole new reality!

Then Jesus made a public spectacle of all the powers and principalities of darkness, stripping away from them every weapon and all their spiritual authority and power to accuse us. And by the power

*of the cross, Jesus led them around as prisoners in a procession of
triumph. He was not their prisoner; they were his!*
Col 2:15

This is what I believe is on Jesus' heart for you as I write this key. He
wants to flood the eyes of your heart, undergirding and strengthening
you with fresh, powerful, revelation-light. He wants to take you by the
hand and bring you into the freedom He secured for you through His
death and resurrection. That is His promise for you, your family and all
those you care about.

Let's step through the doorway of His Word. Be expectant. What you
are about to experience will also bring you into a whole new reality!

If the Son sets you free, you will be free indeed.
John 8:36 (NIV)

*That evening, the disciples gathered together. And because they were
afraid of reprisals from the Jewish leaders, they had locked the doors
to the place where they met. But suddenly Jesus appeared among them
and said, "Peace to you!" Then he showed them the wounds of his
hands and his side—they were overjoyed to see the Lord with their
own eyes!*

*Jesus repeated his greeting, "Peace to you!" And he told them, "Just
as the Father has sent me, I'm now sending you." Then, taking a deep
breath, he blew on them and said, "Receive the Holy Spirit. I send you
to preach the forgiveness of sins—and people's sins will be forgiven.*

But if you don't proclaim the forgiveness of their sins, they will remain guilty."

John 20:19-23

When looking into the Hebrew meaning of the word 'forgiveness', I discovered that one of the root words is 'nasa'. This word carries great power, it means to fully remove, acquit, to completely lift off. Lets re-read John 20:19-23 through the lens of this understanding;

Then, taking a deep breath, he blew on them and said, "Receive the Holy Spirit." I send you to preach the forgiveness of sins—and people's sins will be forgiven. But if you don't proclaim the forgiveness of their sins, they will remain guilty.

John 20:22-23

To His beloved disciples, Jesus imparted the supernatural capacity to speak forth His intention, in order to activate what He had achieved at the cross. Their purpose was to release forgiveness, and consequently, see Holy Spirit lift off Satan's grip and influence that had been present in every person throughout each generation since the beginning of time.

Likewise, Jesus is saying to you now, "Receive what I have done for you. I have completely lifted off all that cascaded down to you through your bloodline since the Fall. You are free! As you share what I have done and release the gift of forgiveness to others also, you too will be a conduit of My authority and power".

I encourage you to stay in this place. Read the verses again slowly, until the full impact of Jesus' words sinks deep into your heart. You are free! Satan's grip and influence have been completely deactivated. You now carry the One who has the authority to unlock every heart around you. You are a carrier of God!

As you simply yield to His Spirit within you by communing and resting, with His Presence as the very strength of your being, supernatural life will become your normal Christian experience.

Jesus yearns for you and everyone your life touches, to experience His love and tangible Presence. He longs for each one to experience New Creation Life, which is accessed through the powerful doorway of forgiveness. Simply put, He wants everyone to experience the truth that He has utterly and irrevocably removed EVERYTHING that separated us from Him, and there is no power in existence able to reverse this!

So now I live with the confidence that there is nothing in the universe with the power to separate us from God's love. I'm convinced that his love will triumph over death, life's troubles, fallen angels, or dark rulers in the heavens. There is nothing in our present or future circumstances that can weaken his love.

There is no power above us or beneath us—no power that could ever be found in the universe that can distance us from God's passionate love, which is lavished upon us through our Lord Jesus, the Anointed

One!

Rom 8:38-39

JOURNAL

Write down your first memory of realising the victory of the cross and experiencing the forgiveness of God. Just as the disciples rejoiced at their moment of discovery that Jesus was alive, recall when you first heard the good news for yourself. Write down the emotions you felt, how it impacted your life, the power and freedom you felt surging through you as you accepted His forgiveness.

Now take everything about that experience and hold it in your heart, and as a prayer, release it over those in your life who Holy Spirit shows you need forgiveness. Whoever He brings to your mind, release your experience of the forgiveness of Christ over them and declare that they are forgiven.

THE BEAUTY OF HOLINESS

"Holiness has made us to be His perfect reflection"

Ephesians 1:4 says, *And he chose us to be his very own, joining us to himself even before he laid the foundation of the universe! Because of his great love, he ordained us, so that we would be seen as holy in his eyes with an unstained innocence.* For these next few, precious moments, as you give Jesus the gift of your full attention, be expectant.

Your desire to reach towards Him, to love Him, to listen and trust that He will speak to you, no matter how tired or compromised you may feel, is His greatest treasure. He will meet you here.

In Ephesians 3:17, Paul gives us insight into the impact of our trust in God. Remember, your capacity to believe is a supernatural gift to you. This gift allows Jesus to enter into your heart and flow into and through your life. It creates the door of access between Jesus, the entire realm of His Kingdom, and you.

No matter how much pain or pressure you face, how exhausted or spiritually weak you may feel right now, this gift remains within you because Christ is within you.

As Jesus shared with us in Matthew 17:20, even faith the size of a tiny mustard seed has within it the power to move mountains because it connects us to God! It's so freeing when we realise that our faith to continue believing isn't dependent on our fluctuating, emotional capability but on His permanent, supernatural gift within. All that He requires from you is your "Yes". Your desire for more will activate His supernatural empowerment.

Then, by constantly using your faith, the life of Christ will be released deep inside you, and the resting place of his love will become the very source and root of your life. Then you will be empowered to discover what every holy one experiences—the great magnitude of the astonishing love of Christ in all its dimensions.

How deeply intimate and far-reaching is his love! How enduring and inclusive it is! Endless love beyond measurement that transcends our understanding—this extravagant love pours into you until you are filled to overflowing with the fullness of God!
Eph 3:17-19

With this understanding fresh in our minds, let's meditate on Ephesians 1:4 as a personal prayer. Allow the supernatural faith within you to open the door and move you towards Jesus. As you do this, let go of all peripheral awareness and focus solely on speaking each word to Him from your heart, choosing to accept that this is God's intention for you.

Drink in the richness of each word's meaning, letting them escort you deeper and deeper into His Presence. Jesus desires for you to experience His immense love for you in this moment, and for you to be secure in the knowledge of your incomparable value to Him.

"Jesus, You chose me to belong to You and united Yourself to me even before the foundations of all creation! Because of Your immense love for me, You ordained me so that You would see me as holy with an unstained purity".

Even before the foundations of the earth were laid, Jesus looked through time and claimed you as His own. He chose you! He knew the exact moment the eyes of your heart would open and you'd see each other face-to-face. He planned the moment when His Spirit would move into you, bathing you with His perfection and you would awaken, entering into the extraordinary life of oneness with Him.

Under the power of Holy Spirit, Paul shares with us in Romans 8:18-19, *I am convinced that any suffering we endure is less than nothing compared to the magnitude of glory that is about to be unveiled within us. The entire universe is standing on tiptoe, yearning to see the unveiling of God's glorious sons and daughters!*

Again, in Ephesians 3 we see how God is teaching His supreme wisdom to every throne and rank of angelic order. He shares the mystery and wonder of His great love and grace, through the revealing of His beloved New Creation!

The purpose of this was to unveil before every throne and rank of angelic orders in the heavenly realm God's full and diverse wisdom revealed through the church.
Eph 3:10

Jesus' brilliant, unfolding plan is irreversible and unchangeable. You have been the desire of His heart before time began. Jesus will never leave you. He will never forsake you. He is with you, in you, always and for the rest of time. You are the object of His love, His living, breathing image! At the cross, Jesus removed everything that Satan embedded into the precious life of mankind, for all time.

You are now holiness itself in Him. You are the display of His glory! Holiness has made us to be His perfect reflection. You are, and forever will be, His beloved New Creation. Your nature is the nature of God; eternal, incorruptible.

Jesus is opening your eyes to comprehend this extraordinary, supernatural reality beyond anything you have known before. He is enabling you to live aligned internally and to express the Beauty of Holiness as your authentic nature. Remember, *The entire universe is standing on tiptoe, yearning to see the unveiling of God's glorious sons and daughters!*

So lean in. Trust in His love for you and let go. Rest in the arms of His holy Presence and allow Him to fill you again. It's your time. You are a 'living word', predestined and chosen to know and reveal Jesus as He unfolds within you the revelation of who He is. The angels are watching and marvelling.

The One who is the Beauty of Holiness is in you and always will be. You are one with Him and He will shine through your life as you believe. This is truly who you are!

JOURNAL

What does it mean for you to know that holiness isn't something you can achieve, but is part of your new nature because it is who He is? What does it look like in your life, to have the Beauty of His Holiness radiating out from you?

Do you see yourself with an unstained innocence? Ask Holy Spirit if there is anything in the way of you accepting this is your true reality. This is how God sees you, so it is who you truly are!

THE DOORWAY INTO GOD'S POWER

"…your impossibility becomes Jesus' opportunity to display His love
and become everything you need Him to be for you"

I n 2 Corinthians 12:9-10, Paul shares with us one of the most powerful truths recorded in scripture. Here we are invited into the promise Jesus gave to Paul, regarding the intense struggles he was enduring. Through this incredible promise, Jesus makes clear Who He wants to be for us in every challenge we face in life.

For a moment, I want us to focus on the final, extraordinary verse; *my weakness becomes a portal.* Any persecution, abuse, torment, lack, sickness, whatever you are facing right now, as you bring it to Jesus, that situation becomes the doorway through which God's immense power enters into your life!

No matter how overwhelming the circumstances, your impossibility becomes Jesus' opportunity to display His love and become everything you need Him to be for you. Let's read this scripture as though Jesus were speaking directly to you. Then let your heart respond as Paul's did.

But he answered me, "My grace is always more than enough for you, and my power finds its full expression through your weakness." So I will celebrate my weaknesses, for when I'm weak I sense more deeply the mighty power of Christ living in me. So I'm not defeated by my weaknesses, but delighted!

For when I feel my weakness and endure mistreatment—when I'm surrounded with troubles on every side and face persecution because of my love for Christ—I am made yet stronger. For my weakness becomes a portal to God's power.

I encourage you to stay here with Jesus for just a little longer. Bring to Him every weakness you face. As you release each struggle and impossibility, look at each one through the lens of this promise. Notice how His strength begins to rise, gently flooding your heart with fresh grace. In this moment, you are moving from natural life (coping in your own strength) to the realm of supernatural living.

As Jesus' power begins to flow, you will become a testimony of hope to the people around you. In the Kingdom of God, this is how our vulnerability becomes an amazing gift to others. Jesus' testimony in your life will become an invitation, a doorway of hope they can step through.

As we move from a place of striving and coping, overwhelmed with pain and oppression, to experiencing the all-sufficient grace of Jesus, you and those you love will likewise be delivered into a place of wholeness and complete, inner rest.

I am convinced that my God will fully satisfy every need you have, for I have seen the abundant riches of glory revealed to me through the Anointed One, Jesus Christ!
Phil 4:19

JOURNAL

What areas feel like a weakness or struggle for you right now? Do you feel like you're still trying to cope in your own strength? Ask Jesus to show you how to let go and surrender those difficulties to Him. Let Him take the lead and be all that you need.

Ask Holy Spirit to remind you of times when your weaknesses became a doorway to His strength and power. Rest in thankfulness and confidence that what He has done before He will do again. There is nothing you can't trust Him with!

AN OASIS OF REST

"He wants to bring you out from all complications and pressures, back
to what matters most; your simple relationship with Him"

I n Matthew 11:28-30, Jesus says to us, *"Are you weary, carrying a
heavy burden? Then come to me. I will refresh your life, for I am
your oasis. Simply join your life with mine. Learn my ways and
you'll discover that I'm gentle, humble, easy to please. You will find
refreshment and rest in me. For all that I require of you will be
pleasant and easy to bear."*

For these next few moments, let go of everything crowding in for your
attention. Breathe in deeply and as you breathe out, roll every pressure
onto Jesus. Turn the attention of your heart onto His face. Listen to
Jesus speaking through every word as you read this scripture again
slowly. Step towards Him into the secret place of His Presence within
you.

Jesus is drawing you deeper into the experience of Him as your oasis.
He is your hiding place, the place where you can just snuggle in and be
safe, where the arms of His Presence lock garrison around you as a
protective shield of love and peace. The authority of Who He is is your
strength and comfort.

*"Are you weary, carrying a heavy burden? Then come to me. I will
refresh your life, for I am your oasis. Simply join your life with mine.
Learn my ways and you'll discover that I'm gentle, humble, easy to*

please. You will find refreshment and rest in me. For all that I require of you will be pleasant and easy to bear."

Jesus wants you to experience Him as the Source and Strength of your life. I can feel Him reaching out to you to refresh you and fill you with joy. He wants to silence the noise and gently reignite your capacity to wholeheartedly believe. He wants to breathe His Spirit into you and bring you into deep, inner rest.

Jesus is right here with you. This is your moment to move forward, stepping out from the place of weariness and carrying burdens, even the burden of trying to live a 'good Christian life'. Jesus wants to lift the weight of your life off you and fill you with peace. He wants to bring you out from all complications and pressures, back to what matters most; your simple relationship with Him.

Stay here for a while longer. Linger in His Presence. Keep your heart's gaze upon Him. Enjoy your life joined to Him! Let your heart rediscover that He is *gentle, humble, easy to please*. Here, you will find the most exquisite, extraordinary, beautiful and fulfilling life. Here, you will find rest.

You will seek me and find me when you seek me with all your heart.
Jer 29:13 (NIV)

JOURNAL

Amongst the busyness of life, do you ever find yourself longing for an oasis of rest? Take this time to be recharged in His Presence and let go of anything He wants you to release to Him.

How can you bring rest more intentionally into your lifestyle? Write down how you can create space to regularly check in with the Lord if there's anything you've picked up that He isn't requiring you to carry. He is your constant oasis, always available.

A LOVER'S PROTECTION

"Your authentic love moves the heart of God and mobilises Heaven on your behalf. Your life is the focus of His attention"

P salm 91:14-16 reads; *"Because you have delighted in me as my great lover, I will greatly protect you. I will set you in a high place, safe and secure before my face. I will answer your cry for help every time you pray, and you will find and feel my presence even in your time of pressure and trouble.*

I will be your glorious hero and give you a feast. You will be satisfied with a full life and with all that I do for you. For you will enjoy the fullness of my salvation!"

When you love Jesus, no matter how weak you may feel, your tiny attempts to please Him and wrap the arms of your heart around Him, not only bring Him great joy but release His sovereign strength and protection over your life. This most privileged of all experiences is also the most powerful choice you will ever make.

In a moment we'll read this scripture again, this time with your full attention on Jesus and what He's saying to you through each word's meaning. As you do this, every promise will begin to open up as a doorway of encounter. As you read this way, notice your heart beginning to stir. Keep the eyes of your heart focused. Stay within the experience of Jesus' love as He begins to envelop you. Thank Jesus for being with you.

Surrender everything you are to Him. As Jesus begins to awaken your love, you will feel Him drawing you nearer and deeper within Himself and filling you with peace. In the stillness of this moment, your heart will begin to receive the fresh breath of understanding, moving into you from Jesus' heart.

With Divine understanding and the experience of God's love beginning to gently flood your senses, your heart will be set free and your life will transform.

"Because you have delighted in me as my great lover, I will greatly protect you. I will set you in a high place, safe and secure before my face. I will answer your cry for help every time you pray, and you will find and feel my presence even in your time of pressure and trouble. I will be your glorious hero and give you a feast. You will be satisfied with a full life and with all that I do for you. For you will enjoy the fullness of my salvation!"
Ps 91:14-16

You have given all that you are to Jesus. Your heart is now His inheritance. It is His most precious gift, therefore, Jesus jealously guards and protects your life. His love for you is constant, unchanging, fierce and eternal. Your authentic love moves the heart of God and mobilises Heaven on your behalf. Your life is the focus of His attention. You carry His beauty and power.

But one is my beloved dove—unrivalled in beauty, without equal, beyond compare, the perfect one, the favorite one. Others see your beauty and sing of your joy. Brides and queens chant your praise: "How blessed is she!" Look at you now—arising as the dayspring of dawn, fair as the shining moon. Bright and brilliant as the sun in all its strength. Astonishing to behold as a majestic army waving banners of victory.

Songs 6:9-10

Jesus wants you to know how He sees you and for you to be confident of His protection. He wants you to watch Him move troubles out of the way as your Strength, your Glorious Hero, reigning as Sovereign King over every aspect of your life. His mighty arms are wrapped as a fortress around your life. Your love for Him makes you powerful!

You stand in victory above the rest, stately and secure as you share with me your vineyard of love.

Songs 7:7

The vineyard of your love (your heart) is the most contested place in the universe. It is the Holy of Holies, the true seat of power. Whatever is enthroned there has access to and influence over your life and everything within it. Let everything that has taken precedence within your heart, anything that holds a place of priority above Jesus, melt away as you stay with Him now for just a few moments longer.

Invite Jesus to be enthroned in your heart. Invite Him to take up full residence as King and Lord of your life. He is your Security and Safety, your Healer and the Lover of your soul. Tell Jesus how much you desire to experience Him meeting your every need. Tell Him how much you long to experience the enjoyment of His love, being free to love Him fully in the way He is worthy; unencumbered by the cares of this life.

He understands your pain. He understands everything about you. He chose you and now you belong to Him. You said "Yes" to the King, to be His beloved Bride, His counterpart forever. No one can snatch you out of His hands!

Now I decree, I will ascend and arise. I will take hold of you with my power, possessing every part of my fruitful bride. Your love I will drink as wine, and your words will be mine.
Songs 7:8

Because you have delighted in me as my great lover, I will greatly protect you. I will set you in a high place, safe and secure before my face.
Ps 91:14

JOURNAL

Write down times when you saw the protection of God in your life. Meditate on your memories of His faithfulness to guard you.

Are there any circumstances where you feel He didn't protect you? Ask Him to show you how He was Protector over you in those situations. Let Him show you what you haven't seen before, so you can fully believe and accept that He truly is your safety and guard.

FACE-TO-FACE

"We don't have to search to find Him but can simply sit down on the inside and gaze"

The extraordinary scripture you're about to read provides us with insight into what has happened and shows us the glory of what Jesus accomplished on the cross. As you begin to read 2 Corinthians 3:18, slowly savouring every word, invite Holy Spirit to release His transforming power through you to flood the eyes of your heart with light and enable you to experience this reality for yourself.

We can all draw close to him with the veil removed from our faces. And with no veil we all become like mirrors who brightly reflect the glory of the Lord Jesus. We are being transfigured into his very image as we move from one brighter level of glory to another. And this glorious transfiguration comes from the Lord, who is the Spirit.

What glory now floods our being and shines forth from within us, as we live in conscious union with our Creator! We see this clearly through the life of Moses, recorded in scripture as the most humble man on the face of the earth, who lived to be with his Lord and walked with Him face-to-face, breath-to-breath.

...and the people of Israel would see the radiant glow of his face. So he would put the veil over his face until he returned to speak with the Lord.
Ex 34:35 (NLT)

In Acts 6, we see Stephen standing falsely accused before the supreme council in Jerusalem, loving Jesus with all his heart, his face shining with the glory of God.

Every member of the supreme council focused his gaze on Stephen, for right in front of their eyes, while being falsely accused, his face glowed as though he had the face of an angel!

Acts 6:15

Also, as Jesus prayed on the Mount of Transfiguration His face began to glow, shining with the brilliant glory-light of God.

As he prayed, his face began to glow until it was a blinding glory streaming from him. His entire body was illuminated with a radiant glory. His brightness became so intense that it made his clothing blinding white, like multiple flashes of lighting.

Luke 9:29

As they did, so will we!

Remember Paul's glorious words to us in Galatians 2:20, *And now the essence of this new life is no longer mine, for the Anointed One lives his life through me—we live in union as one!*

All we need to do now is simply turn our attention and affection back onto Him, lifting our gaze onto the face of God, positioning ourselves to be drenched in the light of His glory. From this place we begin to reflect as in a mirror, the very Person of the Lord Jesus Christ.

Holy Spirit is flooding the eyes of our hearts with understanding. He's awakening us to not only comprehend with our minds by rejoicing in stories from long ago but to know how to continually experience the glorious gospel with all of our hearts. We are waking up to realize what the cross actually accomplished as He brought us forth, His master, third-day creation; His reflection!

How much greater can our experience be under the New Covenant, as Christ Himself dwells in each of us and the veil of deception that separated us from Him no longer exists?

In Luke 10:41-42 (NIV) Jesus said, (I'm sure very tenderly and with great warmth), *"Martha, Martha... you are worried and upset about many things, but few things are needed—or indeed only one. Mary has chosen what is better, and it will not be taken away from her"*.

Sitting at the feet of Jesus and longing above all to know Him, gazing intently, with our full attention on every word He speaks and each expression of His heart, is the better way.

Humbling ourselves and loving Him with all we can give, is the life we are now privileged to live. We don't have to search to find Him but can simply sit down on the inside and gaze. As you choose Jesus, your ability to live from this place will not be taken away from you.

From here you will increasingly shine, reflecting the very nature of God everywhere you go. This is what Moses and Stephen experienced, along with countless others who have gone before us. Jesus walked the earth to show us the way and model this glorious life of transfiguration, and it is yours to step into right now until the end of time. It will not be taken away from you.

JOURNAL

We can easily disqualify ourselves from an intimate relationship with Jesus when He has actually already qualified us! He has made you worthy for oneness with Him. Ask Holy Spirit to show you what He wants your relationship to look like and what He wants to do through your life.

WHAT MATTERS MOST

"Jesus wants you to be captivated and enthralled by the unfolding mystery of His Person, strengthened by His majesty and compelled by His love for you and others!"

G alatians 6:15 encapsulates the most important value for our lives. Here, Pauls tells us, *The only thing that really matters is living by the transforming power of this wonderful new creation life*. In Colossians 1:26-27, Paul writes;

There is a divine mystery—a secret surprise that has been concealed from the world for generations, but now it's being revealed, unfolded and manifested for every holy believer to experience. Living within you is the Christ who floods you with the expectation of glory! This mystery of Christ, embedded within us, becomes a heavenly treasure chest of hope filled with the riches of glory for His people, and God wants everyone to know it!

Let this life-transforming reality sink deeply into your heart; living within you now is the Christ! Jesus Himself is the Transforming Power of your *wonderful new creation life*. He is the Treasure Chest within you! Jesus has made the way for you to experience this new life every single day. This *heavenly treasure chest of hope filled with the riches of glory for His people,* is now your inheritance.

As we look at how Jesus is recorded for us within the Gospels, we get a glimpse into what's available to us as we live in union with Him. He has made it possible for you to live as one with Him in thought and heart: one nature, one mind, able to express Christ through you in every moment from a heart fully content in His love.

Jesus wants you to be captivated and enthralled by the unfolding mystery of His Person, strengthened by His majesty and compelled by His love for you and others!

So they rolled away the heavy stone. Jesus gazed into heaven and said, "Father, thank you that you have heard my prayer, for you listen to every word I speak. Now, so that these who stand here with me will believe that you have sent me to the earth as your messenger, I will use the power you have given me." Then with a loud voice Jesus shouted with authority: "Lazarus! Come out of the tomb!"
John 11:41-43

Then Jesus took the five loaves and two fish, gazed into heaven, and gave thanks to God. He broke the bread and the two fish and distributed them to his disciples to serve the people—and the food was multiplied in front of their eyes!

Everyone had plenty to eat and was fully satisfied. Then the twelve disciples picked up what remained, and each of them ended up with a basket full of leftovers! Altogether, five thousand families were fed that day!
Mark 6:41-44

Just then Jesus turned around and looked at her and said, "My daughter, be encouraged. Your faith has healed you." And instantly she was healed!
Matt 9:22

As I'm writing, I can feel Jesus' protective heart towards you, wanting to remove every remaining area of bondage or sickness that is trying to hold onto your life.

If you're struggling with unbelief, He wants to pour fresh faith into you. If you're struggling with fear, He wants to envelop you in fresh love. Jesus wants your entire being in a state of rest; body, soul and spirit. He wants you sleeping in the midst of the storm, experiencing Him in the boat of your life. He desires for you to be free, healed and filled with peace.

Living within you is the Christ! He's not out there in some unreachable place. The Kingdom of God is within you. What power radiates from your life when this reality and awareness switches on? So let's step in.

Focus your gaze as you read Colossians 1:26-27 again slowly, this time thanking Jesus for His indwelling Spirit. Be expectant for His wisdom to wash through you, causing life-changing truths to upload into your conscious awareness.

Wait on Him for revelation. He will flood the eyes of your heart with understanding. In this place, your strength will be renewed and healing will begin to flow into your emotions. As your mind becomes immersed in truth and your emotions become whole by the kiss of unfolding revelation, even biochemical cascades will begin to release through your physical body. The Greater One lives in you!

There is a divine mystery—a secret surprise that has been concealed from the world for generations, but now it's being revealed, unfolded and manifested for every holy believer to experience. Living within you is the Christ who floods you with the expectation of glory! This mystery of Christ, embedded within us, becomes a heavenly treasure chest of hope filled with the riches of glory for His people, and God wants everyone to know it!

Col 1:26-27

Stay with Jesus now, say "Yes" to His desire to saturate you with His glory. Spend just a few moments longer meditating on His Presence within you. He's removing everything that's oppressing your life and trying to resist your relationship with Him. Invite Jesus to be the Gatekeeper of your access into His Presence from this moment onwards.

As you feel Him, yield and allow Him to take you deeper. Let go of this world for just these few, brief moments and you will begin to experience freedom, bliss and the ecstatic joy of your union with Him.

Come with me through the archway of trust.

Songs 4:8

For God alone has become my Savior. He alone is my safe place; his wrap-around presence always protects me. For he is my champion defender; there's no risk of failure with God.

Ps 62:1-2

JOURNAL

As you read this chapter, what did you feel Jesus detaching from your life?

What came to mind as areas you need Him to fill? He is Healer, Provider, Deliverer, Comforter, Resurrector.

Ask Jesus what it will look like for Him to be whatever is lacking in your life. He isn't far away but closer than your breath!

SUPERNATURAL PEACE

"Peace is the Person of God releasing His supreme Presence, completely removing the authority of the enemy that has attached chaos to your life"

R omans 16:20 says, *And the God of peace will swiftly pound Satan to a pulp under your feet! And the wonderful favor of our Lord Jesus will surround you.* As I write, I can feel Jesus rising on your behalf as your strong, Covenant Partner. I can see Him fastening a thick, supportive, supernatural belt of truth tightly around your waist.

He knows the oppression you face and is releasing fresh grace and strength within you to remember that all you need do is rest. As you become still on the inside, settling into the strength of His Presence, you will begin to experience the deliverance of your King! As fear and anxiety begin to give way to supernatural peace, the deafening sound of your faith will rise in the spirit realm, declaring the Presence of Jesus to your enemy.

Your supernatural trust in the Lord of Heaven's Armies causes your enemy to retreat and disengage his purposes.

I can see you with your head tilted back, laughing with inexpressible joy and gratitude. I see you laughing the way Father does as He sits in victory, enforcing the final rule of Golgotha on your behalf!

Look at how the power brokers of the world rise up to hold their summit as the rulers scheme and confer together against Yahweh and his Anointed King, saying: "Let's come together and break away from the Creator. Once and for all let's cast off these controlling chains of God and His Christ!" God-Enthroned merely laughs at them; the Sovereign One mocks their madness!

Then with the fierceness of his fiery anger he settles the issue and terrifies them to death with these words: "I myself have poured out my King on Zion, my holy mountain. "I will reveal the eternal purposes of God. For he has decreed over me, 'You are my favored Son. And as your Father I have crowned you as my King Eternal... Your domain will stretch to the ends of the earth. And you will shepherd them with unlimited authority.

Ps 2:2-9

In the Hebrew language, the word for peace is the word 'shalom'. As we look at the pictograph for each Hebrew letter, we discover another very important layer of meaning that this word carries. Literally translated it means, "destroying the authority that attaches to chaos".

Seeing Jesus as the Prince of Peace through the lens of this understanding, we see how powerful peace actually is. Peace is the Person of God releasing His supreme Presence, completely removing the authority of the enemy that has attached chaos to your life. His peace mounts garrison over your heart and mind.

His Presence within becomes your protective force-shield calming every storm, soothing away all fear and removing every attempt of the enemy to inflict damage.

This is the same Jesus that rebuked the wind and the waves, who calmed the storm, who raised Jairus' daughter from the dead. This is the same Jesus who clothed Mary and the woman caught in adultery with dignity, who healed their hearts and restored their lives, who continues to this day to heal the blind, the lame and the lepers. The same Jesus who walks on water and moves through walls. The One who created all that is and ever will be, is your God of Peace!

Jesus hung on the cross and rose from the grave and now is with you, in you and for you forever. His love and favour wrap around your life as a protective, impenetrable shield of power, enforcing His rule on your behalf for all time! Worship Him not only as the Lover of your soul but as your Eternal King of Glory!

He is for you, therefore no weapon will ever be formed against you that can prosper. Every tongue that has ever risen in judgement against you is condemned. You are blessed and highly favoured in life because you belong to Him!

Open your heart and listen for His songs of deliverance. He is bringing you to live high above the noise of the enemy. He is sensitising you to experience the place you occupy on earth alongside your King in Heaven. He rules and now through His power, so do you!

He raised us up with Christ the exalted One, and we ascended with him into the glorious perfection and authority of the heavenly realm, for we are now co-seated as one with Christ...We have become his poetry, a re-created people that will fulfill the destiny he has given each of us, for we are joined to Jesus, the Anointed One.

Eph 2:6,10

JOURNAL

What times in your life have you seen Jesus, your Prince of Peace, crush the enemy under your feet? Meditate on these experiences and let faith rise within you. I invite you to share these testimonies with others as it will encourage your faith as well as theirs.

What is the song of deliverance that He is singing over you today? Join Him in His sound and celebrate the victory He has already won for you!

TRANSFORMATIVE BELIEFS

"He is our true nature and He wants us to live powerfully, free from all toxic thinking, as living testimonies of hope who showcase the New Creation reality!"

Proverbs 23:7 (AMPCE) reads, *As a man thinks in his heart, so is he.* During the last couple of decades, leading experts from the neuroscientific community have researched the effect of spiritual practices on the brain. As they've observed the different neurological networks that are active during meditation and prayer, the results have shown a significant improvement in the overall well-being of the practitioner.

A growing number have begun to share their breakthrough findings and some conclude that believing in a God of Love unquestionably changes our brain chemistry and brings healing to our bodies. This results in us operating from our highest-functioning neurological and biochemical state.[1]

Clearly, what we believe affects every aspect of our lives. Our beliefs form our values and then the worldview we live out of. This affects our experiences in life on every level and eventually creates our external reality. Everything we do, every decision we make, every interaction we have, are all shaped by our beliefs.

---

[1] For deeper study, read 'How God Changes Your Brain: Breakthrough Findings from a Leading Neuroscientist' By Andrew Newberg, M.D., Mark Robert Waldman, ©2009, Ballantine Books, New York, USA.

Science is proving the wisdom of the scriptures, that believing in God is critical for our overall well-being; body, soul and spirit. Our physical being reflects the truth that we were created by Him for Divine union. Remaining in the deception of separation and holding onto thoughts and attitudes of heart that are not authored by God, brings degeneration into our physical bodies.

We were created by Jesus to live in relationship with Him, in intimate union. Any other way of life is to remain in a distorted expression, contrary to God's original intention. Apart from Him, we begin to die.

"I cannot afford to have a thought in my head about me that is not in His"

- Bill Johnson

Through Jesus' indwelling Spirit, we have access to His mind and can know His thoughts on all matters in life. As we learn to draw on Him, communing with Him and increasing our God-consciousness, we access the true Source of Life. With practice, this eventually becomes as natural to us as breathing. All sense of separation or distance and the resulting trauma this can induce, eventually disappears.

Jesus wants us to know His thoughts, particularly concerning ourselves; who we are and Whose we are. He created us to live as secure and confident expressions of Himself. He is our true nature and He wants us to live powerfully, free from all toxic thinking, as living testimonies of hope who showcase the New Creation reality! When we live this way, it enables others to remember who they are.

I pray that the light of God will illuminate the eyes of your imagination, flooding you with light, until you experience the full revelation of the hope of his calling—that is, the wealth of God's glorious inheritances that he finds in us, his holy ones!

Eph 1:18

Invite Jesus to step into your conscious awareness and create new beliefs in your heart. Through new encounters with Him, Jesus will drown out the experiences you lived through which created beliefs that have held you in some level of captivity. Scoop up your thought life collectively, bundling it all into your arms and hand the whole lot over to God.

Breathe in and out deeply. Relax. Let go. Begin to thank Jesus for His Presence residing within you. See Him before you with outstretched arms, kindness and love shining from His eyes and entirely engulfing you in light.

In a moment we will look at Psalm 139. Read each verse slowly, sitting in His Presence and speak directly to Him. As you begin to sense Him, pause and stay there in the experience. Let the expression of your heart rise freely to Him. When His Presence seems to gently lift, move to the next verse.

Listen for His gentle whispers as your heart reaches for connection. With a single focus, stay fully present. Jesus' Presence is always in the present moment!

As you fully give yourself to Him with undivided attention, you will find that you are no longer here but you are lost in Him. In this place, you have moved from desire, devotion and contemplation, into experiencing the bliss of union. This is where our hearts are healed in a moment and our beliefs change as the overriding experience of God transforms us.

Lord, you know everything there is to know about me. You perceive every movement of my heart and soul, and you understand my every thought before it even enters my mind. You are so intimately aware of me, Lord. You read my heart like an open book and you know all the words I'm about to speak before I even start a sentence!

You know every step I will take before my journey even begins. You've gone into my future to prepare the way, and in kindness you follow behind me to spare me from the harm of my past. With your hand of love upon my life, you impart a blessing to me. This is just too wonderful, deep, and incomprehensible!

Your understanding of me brings me wonder and strength. Where could I go from your Spirit? Where could I run and hide from your face? If I go up to heaven, you're there! If I go down to the realm of the dead, you're there too! If I fly with wings into the shining dawn, you're there! If I fly into the radiant sunset, you're there waiting! Wherever I go, your hand will guide me; your strength will empower me.

It's impossible to disappear from you or to ask the darkness to hide me, for your presence is everywhere, bringing light into my night. There is no such thing as darkness with you. The night, to you, is as bright as the day; there's no difference between the two. You formed my innermost being, shaping my delicate inside and my intricate outside, and wove them all together in my mother's womb.

I thank you, God, for making me so mysteriously complex! Everything you do is marvelously breathtaking. It simply amazes me to think about it! How thoroughly you know me, Lord! You even formed every bone in my body when you created me in the secret place, carefully, skillfully shaping me from nothing to something. You saw who you created me to be before I became me!

Before I'd ever seen the light of day, the number of days you planned for me were already recorded in your book. Every single moment you are thinking of me! How precious and wonderful to consider that you cherish me constantly in your every thought! O God, your desires toward me are more than the grains of sand on every shore! When I awake each morning, you're still with me.

Ps 139:1-18

JOURNAL

As you read this chapter, what powerful, healthy thoughts did Holy Spirit begin stirring within you? Spend some time meditating on the transformative beliefs and perspectives that Jesus has revealed to you and let them flood through your mind.

REFLECTING GOD

"You are destined to be His perfect reflection, to overcome and co-reign with Jesus"

In Song of Songs 6:3-4, we are given a glimpse into the extraordinary life made available to us through our intimacy with Jesus. Here, we are given further insight into who we are and who we are becoming, as we forsake all others and embrace our union with Him. This scripture extends to us a holy invitation into the deeper life.

The wisest choice we will ever make in our lives is to prioritise our relationship with Jesus.

Portrayed for us through these verses, we see that all life, fulfilment and power flow from this place, which is what the enemy fears the most! As you step through this doorway of revelation, you enter into everything Jesus now proclaims you to be. His transforming strength will begin to enfold you and ignite your heart.

You will know, in the very core of your being, that this is YOU. It's who you truly are in His strength!

This scripture contains transforming power. It is a supernatural door that only God can open and no man, nor demonic spirit, can ever shut. His purposes for you are untouchable. All of Heaven is invested in your well-being.

I am my beloved's and my beloved is mine; he browses among the
lilies.
You are as beautiful as Tirzah, my darling, as lovely as Jerusalem, as
majestic as troops with banners.
Songs 6:3-4 (NIV)

In her famous commentary on Song of Songs, written in the early 1680s, Madame Jeanne Guyon opens up a little further, the rich treasures of revelation held within these verses. She writes;

"Jesus has adorned you with all that is His and has made you a co-heir of His inheritance. You are a worthy dwelling place for Him, and you desire Him to dwell in you. As beautiful as you are to Christ, you are frightening to the devil. Sin is threatened by your presence. Your enemies flee from you, though you do not even strike one blow.

The enemies of God fear you because you are united with Him. Pity those who fight their entire lives and achieve no victory! If we give ourselves to God, abandoning ourselves to him we will become more formidable an opponent than an army ready for war". [2]

I want to draw your attention to that last sentence. Let's read each word again very slowly, this time applying it personally and as a proclamation of truth. As you speak directly to Jesus, expect Him to

---

[2] Jeanne Guyon, 'Song of Songs', Ch 6, 1983 edition. Originally translated from the French by James W. Metcalf, M.D.

move within you in response. Invite Him to fill you again with His beautiful, powerful Spirit.

If you give yourself to God right now, abandoning yourself to Him, leaning completely in full dependency on Him as your very life, you will begin to experience His love beyond anything you've known before. Your surrendered, trusting heart will be overtaken by Perfect Love.

Declare these words: "If I fully give myself to You and abandon myself completely to You, Jesus, I 'will become more formidable an opponent than an army ready for war'. My enemies fear me in this place because I am united to You!".

The Living God is residing within you and you have yielded to the supremacy of His headship as King and Lord of your life. His power now flows freely through you. All sin and darkness have lost control. With one sharp and final blow enacted by your free will, they've lost their ability to gain access to you or this realm through the doorway of your life.

You have now entered the deeper experience of mystical union; one heart, one mind, one Spirit. Every part of you is given over to Jesus.

In this place, you lean as the Shulamite did in Song of Songs, having learned the power of the surrendered life. Here, you become love. Here, you become a perfect reflection of God on the earth. Here, you become untouchable! You are now beginning to drip God and radiate

His beauty. You are a shining one, coming forth in supernatural power, co-reigning with Christ, His nature flooding out from you in every situation.

Stay with Him. Go deeper and deeper through the doorway of His Word.

Prioritise Him. This is His heart's invitation. He is reaching out to you, calling you to sit at His feet as a lifestyle and posture of the heart. As you're leaning, listening, gazing, with the eyes of your heart focusing on Jesus as His love cascades in and through you, He will give you the grace to change. This is the most important decision you will ever make.

Will you go even deeper? Will you put away everything that has competed for His place within your heart? This is your moment. You are destined to be His perfect reflection, to overcome and co-reign with Jesus. The King is held captive by your beauty!

"We have the assurance that where He is enthroned in the heart, His humility and gentleness will be one of the streams of living water that flow from within us"
- Andrew Murray

Declare these words over yourself;

"Jesus has adorned [me] with all that is His and has made [me] a co-heir of His inheritance. [I] am a worthy dwelling place for Him, and

[I]desire Him to dwell in [me]. As beautiful as [I am] to Christ, [I am] frightening to the devil. Sin is threatened by [my] presence. [My] enemies flee from [me], though [I] do not even strike one blow.

The enemies of God fear [me] because [I am] united with Him. Pity those who fight their entire lives and achieve no victory! If [I] give [myself] to God, abandoning [myself] to him [I] will become more formidable an opponent than an army ready for war". [text added]

Meditate on the following verses and let them sink deeply into your heart. This is who you truly are. You always were in the heart of God and now always will be, the beloved Bride of Jesus Christ!

Who could ever find a wife like this one—she is a woman of strength and mighty valor! She's full of wealth and wisdom. The price paid for her was greater than many jewels. Her husband has entrusted his heart to her, for she brings him the rich spoils of victory. All throughout her life she brings him what is good and not evil.

She searches out continually to possess that which is pure and righteous. She delights in the work of her hands. She gives out revelation-truth to feed others. She is like a trading ship bringing divine supplies from the merchant.
Prov 31:10-14

She wraps herself in strength, might, and power in all her works. She tastes and experiences a better substance, and her shining light will not be extinguished, no matter how dark the night... Bold power and glorious majesty are wrapped around her as she laughs with joy over

the latter days.

Prov 31:17-18, 25

"There are many valiant and noble ones, but you have ascended above

them all!" Charm can be misleading, and beauty is vain and so quickly

fades, but this virtuous woman lives in the wonder, awe, and fear of the

Lord.

She will be praised throughout eternity.

Prov 31:29-30

JOURNAL

Ask Jesus to show you how deeply He loves you and how terrifying you are to the enemy because of your intimacy with Him! Meditate on the victorious position He has placed you in, completely surrounded by His protection.

From this perspective, look at the circumstances of your life and ask Jesus to escort you into deeper intimacy with Him in every area. Remember the work of His Spirit is to bring you into the fullness of truth and to saturate you in His transforming glory. He is bringing you forth as His perfect reflection. Your life is His story!

ABOUT THE AUTHOR

Liz Wright is an international speaker, mentor, author, member of the British Isles Council of Prophets, and host of the Charisma podcast show, Live Your Best Life with Liz Wright.

Liz's life changed forever in 1995 through a physical visitation from Jesus Christ. This transformative experience, along with many other encounters throughout the last twenty years, gave her an insatiable hunger to live constantly connected to God's presence. Now she is passionate about facilitating others into the same oneness with Holy Spirit. She lives to help people from every walk of life become confident, powerful and whole, as they experience the Lord's love for themselves.

When Liz is not traveling the globe, she can be found at home with her husband Wesley in the beautiful English countryside. Connect with Liz on Facebook, Instagram and YouTube. Live Your Best Life is available on the Charisma Podcast Network, iTunes, Google Podcasts, Spotify and YouTube.

OTHER BOOKS BY LIZ WRIGHT

EKKLESIA RISING - Visitations From Jesus Revealing the Truth & Power Of Who We Really Are

"I truly believe that reading this book your life will never be the same. Every word is imbued with the Presence of Jesus and has been birthed through supernatural encounter." Wendy Alec.

Available in Paperback and Kindle on Amazon. Audiobook available on lizwright.org

Where life's challenges, the brokenness in others or the enemy's lies have defined you and held you captive, as you read the heart and wisdom of Jesus contained within these pages, the eyes of your understanding will be flooded with light. You will become empowered to experience a level of freedom and peace you never thought possible. With a renewed security in the absolute love of God, you will be set free to live out of your authentic self and so begin to produce your highest purpose.

We are rising out of the ashes of pain and powerless religion, becoming a pure reflection of God in the earth. Destined to be fully filled with His beautiful, powerful Spirit we are together, an emerging unstoppable force of love and transforming authority. A people the realm of darkness cannot prevail against.

E-COURSES & SOAKING AUDIOS

SECRETS OF THE SECRET PLACE

An 8 session series with Liz, activating you into the simple enjoyment and overcoming power of a life beholding the face of Jesus.

What's Included:

- 8 streaming on-demand video lessons
- A full 8 chapter course workbook
- 8 downloadable mp3 soaking prayer activations to lead you into simple and easy abiding in the secret place

View the course on lizwright.org. **Soaking audio activations** are also available separately.

EKKLESIA RISING

In this 4 week course, break free from bondage and be activated into a level of peace and liberty that you may have never thought was possible! Living insecure and without the awareness of Jesus' Presence will become a distant memory.

What's included:

- 20 on-demand video lessons
- Ekklesia Rising audiobook
- Course workbook

- 4 downloadable mp3 activations of prayer to soak in and activate your spirit

View the course on lizwright.org. **Soaking audio activations** are also available separately.

KEYS FOR NEW CREATION LIVING

Keys For New Creation Living Parts 1 & 2 contain a total of 50 Scripture-based soaking audios that are around 4-5 minutes each. They are perfect for your daily time with Jesus to simply soak and receive.

Available on lizwright.org

"As you listen to each audio, you will begin to receive fresh empowerment to truly rise up and live in the fullness of who you are now as a new creation in Christ. You will rise up in fresh strength to walk fulfilled and free in an uninterrupted Union with the Living God." - Liz Wright

Printed in Great Britain
by Amazon

50044676R10111